SOUTHWESTERN INDIAN ARTS & CRAFTS

by Tom Bahti and Mark Bahti

Tom Bahti   The late Tom Bahti, a graduate in anthropology from the University of New Mexico, started in the Indian arts business in 1949. He was nationally recognized as an authority on the arts, crafts, and culture of Southwestern Indians. He was also deeply involved in the future of the people of the Southwest.

Mark Bahti   Mark Bahti, like his father, has authored a number of books and operates an Indian arts shop in Tucson, Arizona. He is active in several Indian-run organizations that seek to provide educational and economic development opportunities for members of the Indian community.

INDEX

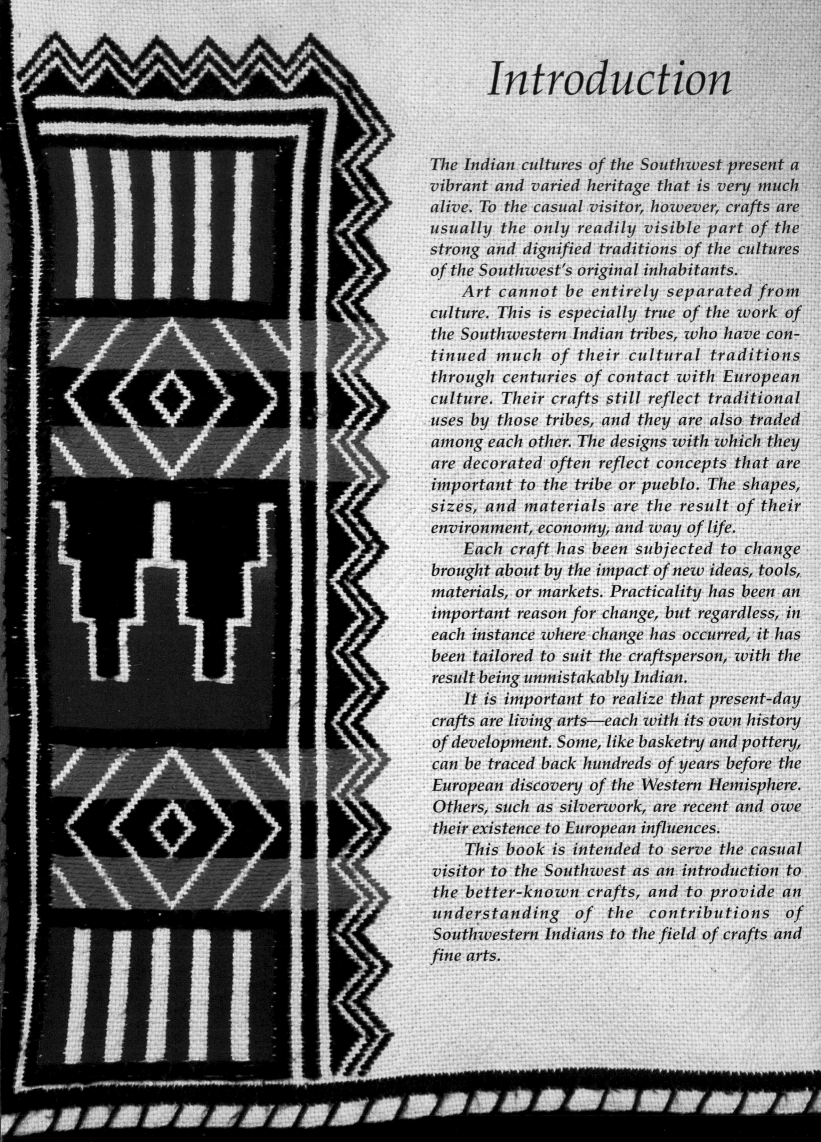

Introduction

The Indian cultures of the Southwest present a vibrant and varied heritage that is very much alive. To the casual visitor, however, crafts are usually the only readily visible part of the strong and dignified traditions of the cultures of the Southwest's original inhabitants.

Art cannot be entirely separated from culture. This is especially true of the work of the Southwestern Indian tribes, who have continued much of their cultural traditions through centuries of contact with European culture. Their crafts still reflect traditional uses by those tribes, and they are also traded among each other. The designs with which they are decorated often reflect concepts that are important to the tribe or pueblo. The shapes, sizes, and materials are the result of their environment, economy, and way of life.

Each craft has been subjected to change brought about by the impact of new ideas, tools, materials, or markets. Practicality has been an important reason for change, but regardless, in each instance where change has occurred, it has been tailored to suit the craftsperson, with the result being unmistakably Indian.

It is important to realize that present-day crafts are living arts—each with its own history of development. Some, like basketry and pottery, can be traced back hundreds of years before the European discovery of the Western Hemisphere. Others, such as silverwork, are recent and owe their existence to European influences.

This book is intended to serve the casual visitor to the Southwest as an introduction to the better-known crafts, and to provide an understanding of the contributions of Southwestern Indians to the field of crafts and fine arts.

MARK BAHTI

Acoma potters, long famous for their water jars, storage vessels, and serving bowls, have also developed art pottery such as this plate by Rebecca Lucario—giving life to new design forms which are based upon the old but reflect the individual artist more.

This Hopi Masaw katsina by Clark Tenakhongva is an older style—complete with mineral and vegetal paints—that has been revived by younger Hopi artists who also use actual feathers. It is not only the artist and the collectors who affect what is produced. Federal regulations prohibiting the use of most types of bird feathers in items to be sold forced Hopi katsina carvers to make wooden feathers.

Corn is the most important crop of the Pueblo peoples. Its significance is seen even in contemporary pottery such as this piece by Bea Tioux from Tesuque.

Though machine-made copies and foreign imitations plague them, Indian artists like Navajo Alex Beeshligaii take pride and satisfaction in continuing to create fine handmade work.

Aesthetics and Economics

"It's nice, but it doesn't look Indian" is a comment, usually made in reference to contemporary work, which reflects less the background of the work than it does the lack of knowledge of the speaker. Indian cultures are not, nor have they ever been, static or stagnant. They are alive and, as such, are continually growing and changing. "Traditional" does not mean better or more authentic—it refers simply to an earlier style or manner. Similarly, "contemporary" or "modern" is simply newer, not less authentic or better. The Navajo squash blossom necklace, an innovation of the 1870s, is now considered a typical piece of very traditional Indian jewelry. Many of the new design concepts, such as the setting of the turquoise on the underside of a bracelet or ring, are likely to be regarded in the future as traditional.

Some buyers of Indian art are of the opinion that commercialism is an evil that ruins or taints Indian art. Their concern whether a piece is "authentic or just made to sell" is one that fails to recognize that all crafts must have an economic basis or they will cease to exist. The craftsperson of any age or culture produces items to use, sell, or trade. When unable to barter labor as a craftsperson, the artisan must seek a livelihood at which a living can be earned. A craft with no market will cease to be created.

Concern whether an item was "made to sell" is often extended to whether it was made for sale to another Indian or to a non-Indian. It implies that if it is made for the non-Indian trade it is somehow less authentic. One would be hard-pressed to find an Indian craftsperson concerned over the cultural identity of the purchaser—the concern is that there *be* a purchaser. The integrity of the work has less to do with the viewer's analysis than the maker's intent.

Even today, comparatively few craftspeople derive most or all of their income from craftwork. Average annual income derived by Indian tribes from their crafts ranges from about 20 percent to less than 1 percent, depending upon the tribe. Economics plays an important role in the survival

of a craft, but it would be a mistake to consider the true value of arts and crafts solely in terms of dollars and cents.

Designs used to decorate Indian crafts can sometimes be identified as representations of clouds, rain, lightning, birds, and the like. Rain obviously plays an important role in traditional Southwestern Indian life, but to assign it a simple meaning like "good luck" or "fertility" is to oversimplify. The pattern on a bracelet or in a rug

Hopi life has changed greatly in this century so it is only natural that those changes would be reflected in their artwork. The Hopi clown katsinas, like this Koshare by Roxie Pela, provide an opportunity for the Hopi to reflect on and satirize such changes.

"Traditional" is a relative term: much of what we think of as traditional Navajo jewelry was new and innovative barely a century ago. Much "modern" jewelry has its roots in the "traditional."

The sculptural form of traditional pottery and the sculptural quality of religious buildings known as kivas were merged in this work by Acoma pottery artist Wilford Garcia.

does not "tell a story." The printed materials that purport to translate or interpret Indian designs are largely spurious. Some dealers in Indian art— Indian and non-Indian—will invent a story to go along with a craft item if they think it will encourage the buyer to make a purchase. (The so-called dream catchers are an example.) Poor craftsmanship cannot be improved by the addition of a colorful story, and fine craftwork will stand on its own merits.

The Individual in Indian Art

Within the craft traditions of each Indian group there has always been room for individual artistic expression. The artisans were known within their small communities, and the notion of signing a piece was unknown. In the last 20 years, however, people buying Indian art and craftwork have become interested in knowing the identity of the artisan, with the result that, where possible, most works are now signed by the maker.

The emergence of the artist as an individual rather than simply as a member of the community has gone hand in hand with the increasing number and economic importance of Indian art exhibitions and competitions, as well as an emerging group of artists who have learned or furthered their art in an academic setting. The work of many of these artists reflects their personal perspectives and interpretations of their world, transcending craft and tribal boundaries. A few even consider their work to be less Indian art than art by Indian artists. Their blazing of new traditions makes it clear that the future of Indian art will be at least as rich and diverse as its past.

Feathers from the Eagle, most powerful of all birds, are revered by most tribes and used in many ways depending upon their beliefs. Indian painters, such as Oliver Enjady, use the feather to symbolize values, traditions, and the power or holiness of the subject matter. These dancers are the Apache Gaan who are the spirits of the mountains and protectors of the Apache and their homeland.

Styles and traditions that are revived can undergo an explosion of experimentation and innovation. A generation ago most pottery at Jemez Pueblo was limited to acrylic-painted sun-dried souvenirs. Since that time traditional pottery-making skills have revived and pottery artists are using those traditions to express their creativity. (From left) Marie R. Romero, Juanita Fragua, Damian Toya, Maxine Toya, Laura Gauchapin, Marie R. Romero, Juanita Fragua

K. C. DEN DOOVEN

Navajo artist Robert Sorrell incorporates designs inside this bracelet. A unique innovation, the technique was pioneered by the late Hopi artist Charles Loloma over 30 years ago.

Although inlay or mosaic work is primarily associated with Zuni Indians, a few Hopi as well as Navajo artists have begun to employ the technique. Spiny oyster shell, once the only source for a red or red-orange inlay material, was replaced by coral from the Mediterranean Sea (and now, the Sea of Japan). In recent years some artists have turned back to spiny oyster shell, as in these two buckles by Alex Beeshligaii. Hammered silver bracelets, an old tradition, have been updated with an ancient hand motif. They are meant to be worn so that the hands are visible atop the wrist.

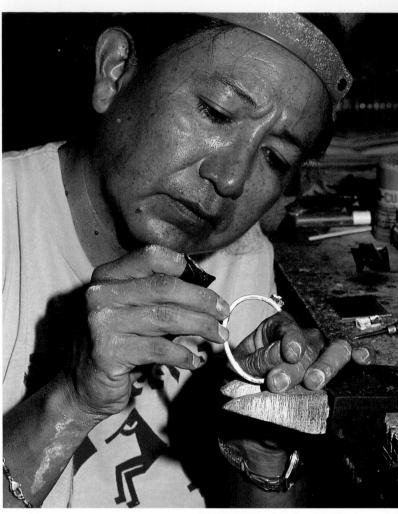

The work of Indian artists, whether on or off the reservation, draws its strength and creativity from the land that shaped and nurtures their ancient cultures.
William Quotskuyva

New materials, new tools, new markets, and new techniques have helped shape Indian jewelry, but artists such as Alex Beeshligaii continue to draw upon the roots of their culture as a vital part of their vision and inspiration. With television, computers, and the growth of the West, Indian tribes are no longer as isolated as they once were. As the range of experiences of Indian artists expands, so does their range of expression, with some drawing more on ancient visions and others drawing on more modern experiences.

Indian art continues to change as Indian life changes. Artists experiment with new images, new perspectives, new techniques, and new materials. A stone Zuni Mountain Lion fetish was the inspiration for this sandcast glass sculpture by Navajo artist Conrad House.

The importance of corn in the modern Indian diet may have diminished somewhat, but its place in Indian religion has not. Accordingly, even as innovation occurs, the corn motif remains strong. Randy Nahohai

In recent years Navajo folk art, itself a relatively new phenomenon, has become popular and encouraged many Navajo to produce pieces carved of sandstone as well as others of wood, metal, and dried, painted mud. Homer Warren

Sculpture is being used by a new generation to express personal creativity and traditional themes. In this alabaster sculpture by Jemez artist Clifford Fragua, the Pueblo dancer appears to be wearing an actual rain cloud instead of a headdress meant to symbolize rain clouds.

Navajo textile artist Isabelle John illustrates a weaver at work among the source of her wool with the weaver's view visible through the warp threads. Navajo weaving has long been a medium for expression of individual creativity. Trains appeared in Navajo rugs about the same time they began to cross Navajoland. Everything from landscapes and fairs to planes, zoo animals, semi-trucks, and cans of soda have appeared in Navajo weaving. Sometimes the expression of personal artistic vision has been as subtle as an unexplained variance in the pattern of asymmetrical use of color.

Indian pottery, whether for storage of food and water, daily use in cooking and serving, or religious uses, has always been created to be beautiful as well as functional. Collectors have prized it for its beauty alone. This bowl by ceramic artist Hubert Candelario from San Felipe illustrates the transition of Pueblo pottery from artistic utility vessel to pure art.

"Five Brothers," a painting by Tewa Indian artist Jordan Harvier, age 12, of Santa Clara Pueblo.

THE NEXT GENERATION OF ARTISTS

As with Indian culture itself, an important strength of Indian art is the teaching of new generations of artists and craftspeople by the older generation. In excavations of prehistoric pueblos archaeologists have not only uncovered some of the objects children played with, but objects they made as well. Works by those learning to perfect their skills have been found alongside those of more accomplished artisans.

Some artists have been trained by both Indian and non-Indian professionals at schools like the Institute of American Indian Art in Santa Fe, founded in 1962. Others have been taught and encouraged in elementary, middle, and high schools across the reservations, as well as in institutes of higher education on and off Indian lands. A number of accomplished Indian artists have made working with Indian children in the schools a priority.

But many still learn at home, usually from an immediate family member. Families take pride in continuing the tradition of artistic excellence, and children develop a sense of pride in themselves and their culture. Art often opens the door to learning more about one's culture. A grandmother instructing a child in the tedious and time-consuming art of basket weaving has time to talk of other things, including traditional stories and the value of keeping the language alive.

Young ceramic artists Brandon and Derek Gonzales learn a pottery tradition made famous by their great-great-grandmother Maria Martinez of San Ildefonso Pueblo.

Painting

Painting on paper is the most recent art expression to be adopted by Indians of the Southwest. Painting itself was practiced long before the Spaniards arrived. Hides, wood, pottery, stones, textiles, kiva walls, even canyon walls were decorated with paints from mineral and vegetal pigments. Artistic works ranged from simple geometrics to very complex, highly stylized, almost abstract designs and naturalistic animal portrayals.

Use of commercial watercolors began in the early 1900s. The pueblo of San Ildefonso produced the first artists in this new medium. Encouraged by painters, collectors, teachers, and anthropologists, many Pueblo Indians began to experiment with watercolor. The earliest depictions were usually ceremonial dancers or daily pueblo activities. In 1932 the U.S. Bureau of Indian Affairs established at the Santa Fe Indian School an experimental class designed to instruct young Native American students in the use of this medium. This led to the development of a popular group of artists whose style came to be known as the Santa Fe School. The program introduced Southwestern Indian painting as a successful new artistic expression in this country and abroad.

Nearly 40 years later the work of this group was criticized as being painted to suit non-Indian patrons. Contemporary artists, many of them graduates of the Institute of American Indian Art in Santa Fe, are now criticized for the same reason by those who prefer the earlier style. Critics on both sides of this controversy fail to recognize the importance of the artist-patron relationship that permits all art to exist. Both sides also fail to give the Indian artists credit for being both individuals and part of a culture that extends back over a thousand years.

Though many contemporary Southwestern Indian artists still use cultural themes in their works, an increasing number have developed personal interpretations and styles incorporating a wide range of media and techniques.

Many contemporary Indian artists attempt to portray the interrelatedness and levels of meaning in traditional Indian life through their paintings.
Oliver Enjady

This painting reflects both the personal artistic vision of the painter, Carl A. Vicenti, and the many aspects of the Jicarilla Apache religious Holiness Rite, a "long-life ritual" sometimes mistakenly referred to as a "Bear Dance."

Religious observances of the Pueblo Indians have long held an interest for the non-Indian, creating a demand for paintings that portray them. As photography and sketching are banned at most ceremonies, demand has increased for such work as this Zuni Shalako portrayal by the late Hopi-Tewa artist Ray Naha.

K. C. DEN DOOVEN

Silverwork

Silverwork, probably the best known of all Indian crafts, is often thought of as an ancient art. However, it is one of the most recent crafts to be adopted by the tribes in the Southwest. Prior to 1850, silver ornaments used by Southwestern Indians were obtained in trade or warfare with other tribes or Spanish settlers.

In the mid-1800s, it was the custom of Mexican *plateros* (silversmiths) from the Rio Grande Valley to roam through Navajo country producing silver trinkets in exchange for livestock. It was from one of these itinerant craftsmen that a Navajo blacksmith named Atsidi Sani, "Old Smith," is believed to have learned the rudiments of silverworking in the early 1850s. In the two decades prior to this time Indian metalworking

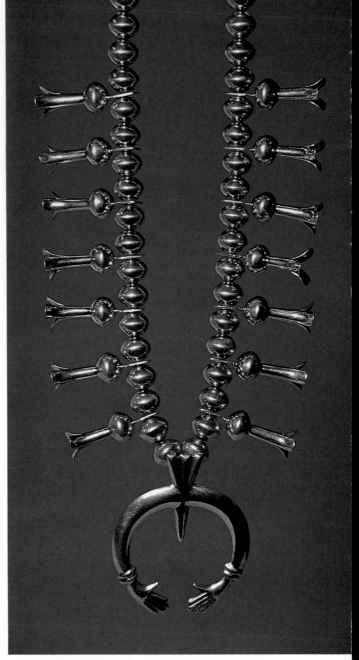

The squash blossom necklace evolved in the late 1800s, as Navajo smiths combined a new technology, silverwork, with Spanish- and Moorish-derived design elements to create a piece of jewelry that is uniquely Navajo. Herbert Coan

Clusterwork—which we think of as typically Zuni—did not begin to evolve until the late 1920s even though the Zunis had been working silver in the late 1800s. Alice Quam

was limited to a few Zuni and Navajo blacksmiths who occasionally fashioned simple items of jewelry from odds and ends of copper and brass.

Frequent raiding by some Navajo bands and continual encroachment on Navajoland by Americans resulted in increased hostilities, which led to a military campaign against the Navajo by the U.S. Army. The Navajo were subjected to a brutal scorched earth policy that culminated in their imprisonment at Bosque Redondo, New

Mexico, far to the southeast of their homeland. During the years of their confinement (1864-68) it appears that more Navajos learned blacksmithing, but the development of silversmithing had halted. Disease and famine swept the tribe, killing one in four and finally forcing the government to admit failure in its attempt to relocate the Navajo. Within a few years of their return, a number of Navajo were working silver.

Hopi silversmithing began in 1892 but the technique of overlay work was not introduced until the 1930s and did not really take hold until after World War II. The Hopi Guild, established in 1949, used the GI Bill to train returning veterans to be silversmiths, using the overlay technique. Today a few Hopi silversmiths use a wide range of techniques, but most rely on the overlay technique, with infrequent use of stones. Antone Honanie

The Indian arts and crafts shops of today are a distinct contrast to the turn-of-the-century shops and reservation trading posts of yesterday. The work found today is truly fine art created by craftspeople working with the latest techniques, tools, and materials. The great variety of work coming from tribes of the Southwest and other areas of the country provides the buyer both items to wear and unique artwork that can be proudly displayed in the home. Where once it was sufficient to know the tribal origins of a piece, now as individual styles flourish, the artist's name and history have become significant. Bahti Indian Arts

15

Indian jewelry is not made solely for the non-Indian collector or tourist. In fact, its earliest and steadiest customers, as late as World War II, were other Indians. Jewelry was the way many Indians carried their wealth. Among the Navajo, jewelry was pawned for loans between lambing and wool-shearing seasons when money was short. With the proceeds from selling lambs or wool, the pieces were then redeemed. The term "pawn" or "dead pawn" refers to some of this older jewelry that was occasionally not redeemed. Pawning ended on the Navajo Reservation in 1976. Today the term has lost most of its significance and does not mean the piece has any especial value or age. A talented Indian silversmith could become a wealthy man. Atsidi Chon, who often traveled to Zuni to make and sell jewelry, is recorded as being able to trade a good, heavy concha belt for a team of matched horses. After a winter of work he would leave Zuni driving sheep, goats, and horses he had acquired in trade.

Navajo sandcasting is one of the oldest silverworking techniques among the Navajo. A stone that is heat resistant yet can be carved with a knife will be cut in half and the surfaces ground smooth before the pattern is carved. A funnel to pour in the silver and tiny channels to let the air out are carved into one surface. Both faces are covered with soot and wired together, then the molten silver is poured. The result is a rough casting that will need trimming, filing, and polishing.

The overlay technique involves sawing the design out of one sheet of silver and then overlaying it on a second sheet to which it is then sweated or soldered. After trimming the edges, the background is darkened with an oxidizing solution before polishing the raised surface. Most Hopi artists use an iron stamp or matting tool to texture the background before oxidizing it.

One of these early silversmiths, Atsidi Chon, "Ugly Smith," traded his work for livestock among the Zuni. He was responsible for teaching his Zuni host, Lanyade, the art of silversmithing about 1872. Interestingly, it was Lanyade who then traded his work among the Hopi and later taught the first Hopi, Sikyatala ("Yellow Light"), silversmithing around 1890.

Two early traders, C. N. Cotton and Lorenzo Hubbell, hired Mexican plateros to teach silversmithing to the Navajos who lived near their trading post at Ganado, beginning in 1884. The arrival of the railroad in the 1890s, and the tourists it brought, increased the demand for Indian jewelry, which motivated more Indians to learn silversmithing. By the early 1920s, the craft had spread eastward to most of the Rio Grande pueblos.

EARLY WORK

The first pieces, fashioned with homemade tools, were often copies of ornaments used by the early Spaniards—among them domed buttons, hollow spherical beads, powder chargers, silver-mounted bridles, loop earrings, and stamped or twisted wire bracelets. Brass and copper, obtained from worn-out utensils, were also used on occasion.

Before Navajo smiths learned to set turquoise, stampwork and file and chisel work were the only ways to decorate their silver jewelry. Stamps were made from any bit of scrap iron, including railroad spikes, old chisels, and broken files.

Silverworking is a relatively new craft among the Tohono O'odham of southern Arizona. This distinctive style with desert motifs began in the mid-1970s with the work of Rick Manuel. Currently there are only a few smiths in the tribe.

The concha belt is one of the earliest styles of jewelry developed by Navajo silversmiths. The oldest had slotted centers through which the leather was strung. This particular style developed just before the turn of the century and continues today.

Many of the styles that evolved were adaptations of jewelry made by the Spanish or the Plains Indians. The decorative nickel-silver disks that hung from the cloth belts of the Plains Indian women became the concha belt. The pomegranate blossoms some Spanish gentlemen wore as trouser or cape ornaments, and the crescent-shaped pendants hung from their horse bridles to ward off the "evil eye," caught the attention of Navajo silversmiths. The crescent-shaped pendant, or *nazha*, was hung on a strand of silver beads. On either side of the pendant were strung several pomegranate blossoms, elongated to suit Navajo aesthetics, to create what became known as a squash blossom necklace, which today is regarded as a very traditional example of Indian jewelry.

Indian silversmiths have long made bracelets for Indian men— who continue to outnumber non-Indian men in wearing bracelets.

Among the early pieces of jewelry, items such as powder chargers and manta pins have disappeared. Others such as the *ketoh,* or bow guard, have survived to be used for different purposes. The ketoh outlived usage of the bow and arrow to become a piece of men's jewelry worn on special occasions. Still others, such as the tobacco canteen, disappeared but were revived. Beginning with a request from a researcher in the 1930s, the canteen is again being made by a few silversmiths for both other Navajo and collectors.

Coins provided the sole source for silver in the early days of silversmithing. American coins were barred from such use in 1890, but Mexican silver pesos—preferred for their higher silver content which made them more malleable—were used as late as 1930, when Mexico forbade their export. Sterling silver (92.5 percent silver, 7.5 percent copper) in slug and ingot form replaced coins, and they in turn were replaced by the late-1940s with ready-made sheet and wire silver, which had been first introduced two decades earlier as part of an effort to increase productivity. At no time did the Indians mine their own silver.

Hopi jewelry draws much of its design inspiration from other crafts, including painted pottery, woven and embroidered textiles, and katsina spirits, as well as the natural world. (Top to bottom) Antone Honanie, Victor Masayesva III, Fernando Puhuhefvaya, Unsigned, Victor Masayesva, Unsigned

One of the biggest bursts of innovation in materials and techniques of jewelry making and design began in the early 1960s with the work of the late Hopi artist Charles Loloma, who created the bracelet at top right. Others, like the Hopi artists who made the other works in this photo, have followed his lead— experimenting with techniques like reticulation, and materials ranging from niobium and titanium to charoite from Siberia and sugilite from the Kalahari.

Over time, objects like silver boxes appeared—this one by Jimmie Herald, Sr.—because the market requested them, while others like bow guards largely disappeared because there was no longer any use for them.

Turquoise was being set by 1880, but its use was rare. Glass, jet, shell, trade beads, and garnets were also tried, but were not popular. Turquoise was used sparingly for the next several decades, though the trader Lorenzo Hubbell imported Persian turquoise for several years in a successful attempt to produce more turquoise and silver jewelry. American turquoise became readily available by the 1920s, with the opening of mines and lapidary shops—all owned and run by non-Indians.

With the exception of mosaic, cluster, and inlay work, most of the turquoise used by Indian silversmiths is purchased already cut and polished. Coral, from the Mediterranean Sea (and now the Sea of Japan), was first imported in the 1930s, and has been used increasingly since the 1950s. Before coral was available artisans relied upon spiny oyster shells, traded from the Pacific Coast of Baja California, for a red-orange material. Artisans now may use stones from virtually anywhere in the world: lapis lazuli from Afghanistan, sugilite from South Africa, charoite from Siberia, and opals from Australia.

New Markets

Until the 1890s most of the silverwork produced was acquired by other Indians. With the appearance of tourists, a new market opened up. Orders from curio companies that catered to the tourists added to their orders items such as napkin rings, salad sets, tie bars, and cuff links. At this time the silversmiths were paid by the ounce, plus so much for each stone set. In order to make the jewelry more affordable for the Eastern buyers, companies requested lighter silverwork from the silversmiths. It should be noted however, that the notion of "heavy, old Navajo silver" does not always square with how the precious and relatively rare metal was used by the early Navajo silversmiths. Some of the heaviest Indian jewelry has been made in the past 20 years. In any event, the weight does not equate with quality.

To fit the Eastern notion of what Indian jewelry should look like, the pieces were decorated with stampwork designs such as crossed arrows, steer heads, and thunderbirds. About this same time a list was created that purported to "interpret" the designs. According to it, a running horse became a symbol of a long journey, and rain clouds of good luck. These "meanings" were concocted for the symbol-minded buyer by

Though best known for their stone and shell jewelry, several artisans from Santo Domingo Pueblo work in silver. These sandcast pendants by Anthony Lovato are based on Pueblo tablita dancers and Pueblo women balancing water jars. They are set with turquoise, orange spiny oyster shell, and purple charoite.

Before a Zuni artisan can begin inlaying stone and shell, a silver frame must be completed. The stone and shell mosaic and inlay work has its roots in a prehistoric tradition of mosaics set on stone and shell. Setting them in silver began about 1930. Leonard Martza

This inlay pendant by Zuni artist Dennis Eedakie is called a spinner since it rotates and has another, equally intricate design on the reverse side. This type of work is judged not only by its aesthetic qualities but also by the quality of the workmanship. In this case the fit is so precise that the stone and shell pieces are separated by less than the thickness of a sheet of paper.

silversmiths and lapidarists are employed (largely in the Gallup, New Mexico area) doing benchwork for an hourly wage or on a piecework basis.

Some people lament the passing of "fine old silverwork." The truth is that more fine silverwork is being produced today than in any period in the past. A wider range of materials are being used, new techniques are being incorporated, and new styles are constantly being introduced. Part of the increase in the quality of the work is the result of new and better tools, but it is primarily the result of continuing efforts by the artisans themselves to improve both design and craftsmanship.

canny merchants responding to questions of "what does it mean?"

Both markets, Indian and non-Indian, continue today, changing as fashion and usage change. A Navajo silversmith may produce a heavy sandcast bracelet for an Anglo customer, but prefer to wear a Zuni bracelet himself. Both may covet an old bracelet, but the Anglo may prize the patina of age while the Navajo wearer is more likely to have it cleaned and brightly polished.

Silversmithing is one of the native crafts at which an artisan, employed full time, can earn a living. However, much of the work produced is still the result of part-time labor, even in cases where the entire family participates in jewelry making. An increasing number of Indian

Zuni jewelry techniques include mosaic, channel, inlay, cluster (the larger stones), needlepoint (the long thin stones), and petitpoint (very tiny, usually round stones). The latter three categories are judged for quality based upon symmetry and consistency.

Turquoise

Turquoise is a semiprecious stone found in many arid regions of the world including the Middle East, China, Australia, and Chile as well as the American Southwest where it has been mined and used for over 1,500 years. In pre-Hispanic times Southwestern Indians mined turquoise with stone hammers and picks made of antler. Fire was used to crack bedrock containing the blue gem. The largest of these early mines was near Cerillos, New Mexico, near present-day Santa Fe. It extended 200 feet underground and was 300 feet wide in places. Turquoise from pre-Columbian mines in the Southwest was widely traded, some traveling as far as the Aztec Empire in Mexico.

Cut turquoise was not readily available in the late 1800s when Indian silversmiths began setting it in their jewelry. The stones used often were broken earrings or pendants from necklaces. For a few years during this period a trader at Ganado, Lorenzo Hubbell, imported turquoise from Persia in order to supply silversmiths in his area. By the 1920s several American turquoise mines were in operation and producing cut stone.

Today turquoise is mined in a number of locations in Colorado, New Mexico, Arizona, Nevada, and northern Mexico. China is also becoming an important source. None of the mines are owned by Indians, and most of the mining is done on a small scale by private individuals or small companies although some turquoise is recovered as a by-product of copper mining. With the exception of inlay, cluster, and mosaic work, most of the stone set in Indian jewelry over the past 75 years has been cut and polished by non-Indians.

Indian jewelry artists have always used the full range of colors in turquoise, sometimes seeking the unusual stone for inspiration and other times looking for a specific type of turquoise to complement their silver design. When multiple stones are used, matching them can become a problem. Additionally, as such a piece is worn, soaps and oils can cause the colors to change at different rates even though the stones may have come from the same mine.

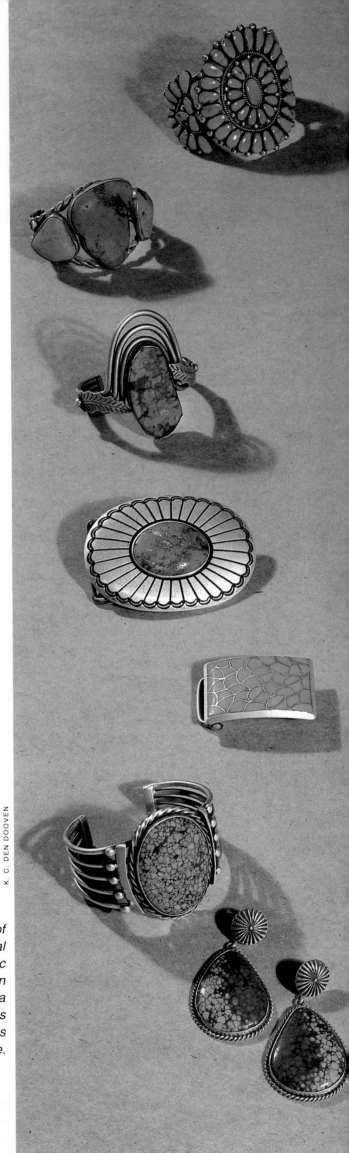

K. C. DEN DOOVEN

The double strand of beads hanging from this multi-strand nugget necklace is called a jocla, *which is a Navajo word meaning simply "earrings." The earrings were once often hung from the bottom of necklaces while riding, lest they be torn from the ear by a tree branch. Eventually they became a design element of the necklace itself, although ones small enough to wear as earrings are still made. The shell beads at the bottom of the jocla are referred to as "corn" because of their resemblance to corn kernels. The style of wrapping at the top of the necklace, usually done with cotton string, predates the use of catches and hooks. It is still popular, however, because it makes wearing a heavier necklace more comfortable.*

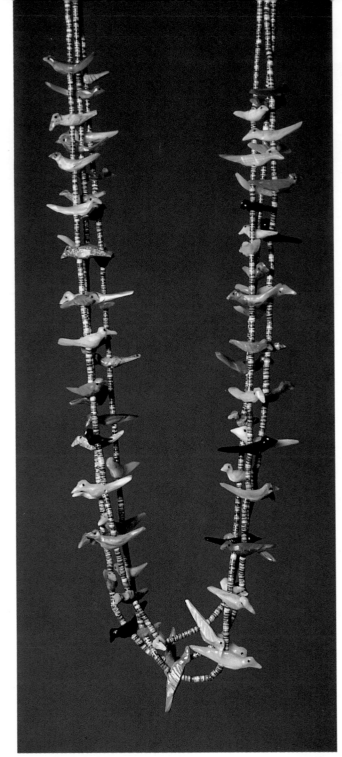

to carve animals that they do not traditionally recognize as fetishes themselves such as owls, frogs, turtles, rabbits, and fish.

The distinction between a carving and a fetish is a fine one, resting less on the intent of the maker than the use of the owner. Even store-bought plastic horses have been adorned with prayer feathers and used as fetishes. The traditional viewpoint is simple: if you believe it is a fetish, it is—if you don't, it isn't, for the spirit within the fetish won't assist an owner who doesn't believe in it.

The most commonly seen fetishes are hunting fetishes, which generally have a small replica of an arrowhead attached. According to some, an arrowpoint can be added simply as an offering, or as protection for the fetish itself as in the case of a livestock fetish. Bits of shell, coral, or turquoise and feathers may be tied to these stone animals to increase their power, or as offerings to the fetish spirits to increase their inclination to honor requests.

This Navajo bison carving by Roy Davis was made from septarian—limestone and quartz crystals—with turquoise horns.

Though called fetish necklaces, in the traditional Zuni sense fetishes cannot be used for jewelry. These are simply animal carvings on a necklace. Prehistoric drilled stone and shell animals found during an excavation in the early 20th century inspired several Zuni to begin making them for sale and trade.

The stone used can contribute as much to the "personality" of a carving as the personal style of the carver. (The two bears with fish would be considered carvings, not fetishes.)

Early fetishes were often carved from stones that already resembled an animal and needed only a little work with a piece of rough sandstone to highlight certain features. Mike Romero

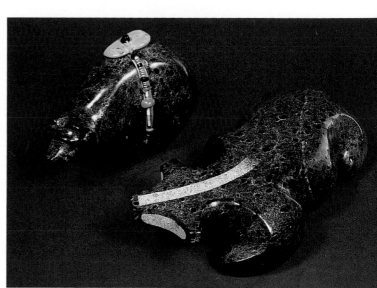

Modern equipment now allows for much greater detail but a steady hand and a good eye are still required. The new equipment means that stones once too hard to work can be carved with relative ease. Mike Romero

Some carvers prefer to work with stones from the traditional boundaries of their land while others actively seek out interesting and unusual stones from around the world. Regardless of materials and tools used, each carver has his or her own distinct style. Mike Romero, from the Tewa Indian pueblo of Santa Clara, not only makes fetishes but also much larger pieces which are intended for use as sculpture.

Overleaf: The Indian art and symbols of the center spread were collected by Tom Bahti over many years of working directly with people of individual tribes in the Southwest. Some elements came from kiva mural paintings excavated by the University of New Mexico, where Tom was a student. Artwork by Tom Bahti, 1962.

PAIUTE

HAVASUPAI

WALAPAI

MOHAVE

WALAPAI

CHEMEHUEVI

YAVAPAI

YAVAPAI - APACHE

MOHAVE-
CHEMEHUEVI

MOHAVE
APACHE

APACHE

PIMA
MARICOPA

TOHONO O'ODHAM

MARICOPA

YUMA

COCOPA

TOHONO O'ODHAM

TOHONO O'ODHAM

HOPI

NAVAJO

INDIAN RES

ARIZONA an

CONTEMPO

JICARILLA

TAOS

PICURIS

SAN JUAN
SANTA CLARA
SAN ILDEFONSO
NAMBE
TESUQUE

JEMEZ   COCHITI
ZIA   SANTO
               DOMINGO
SANTA ANA   SAN FELIPE

SANDIA

ZUNI

ACOMA   LAGUNA

ISLETA

MESCALERO

TIONS of
N MEXICO

DESIGNS

Reservation Area

Navajo Rugs

According to anthropologists, the Navajo learned weaving from the Pueblo Indians—where weaving is done exclusively by the men. By Navajo traditions it was Spiderwoman who first taught Navajo women how to weave. (Only a very few Navajo men practice the craft.) Regardless of origin, it became a vital part of Navajo economic life and culture. Though yarn preparation has changed over the years, the basic weaving technique has been unchanged for centuries. As early as three centuries ago the quality of Navajo weaving was acknowledged; a Spanish territorial governor wrote that Navajo weaving surpassed that of the finest Spanish weavers. Hazel Tallman

Relative newcomers among the Indians of the Southwest, the Navajo entered this region as hunter-gatherers 600 to 800 years ago. Under the influence of the Pueblo Indians many Navajo groups had begun to farm when the Spanish entered the Southwest and introduced both horses and livestock. From them the Navajo obtained sheep, substituting its wool for the cotton with which they had learned from the Pueblo Indians to weave. (According to Navajo tradition it was Spiderwoman who taught them to weave.) Soon

(continued on page 38)

Traditionally the shearing, cleaning, carding, dyeing, and spinning of the wool comprised much of the time necessary to complete a weaving. While Navajo still raise and shear sheep, most weavers now rely upon processed wool which is ready for the final spinning and a few even prefer ready-to-use commercially spun wool. Regardless, the hours before the loom remain unchanged. For over a century non-Navajo experts have predicted the end of Navajo weaving, but the tradition continues to be passed on to new generations of young Navajo women. Though many may never weave much, they carry with them a rich and vital part of Navajo culture. Hazel Tallman

Weaving involves many long hours. For a young woman being taught the art, it becomes an opportunity to learn more than just the technique—it becomes a time to learn more of Navajo traditions and values, becoming a part of the tapestry of Navajo culture. Hazel Tallman

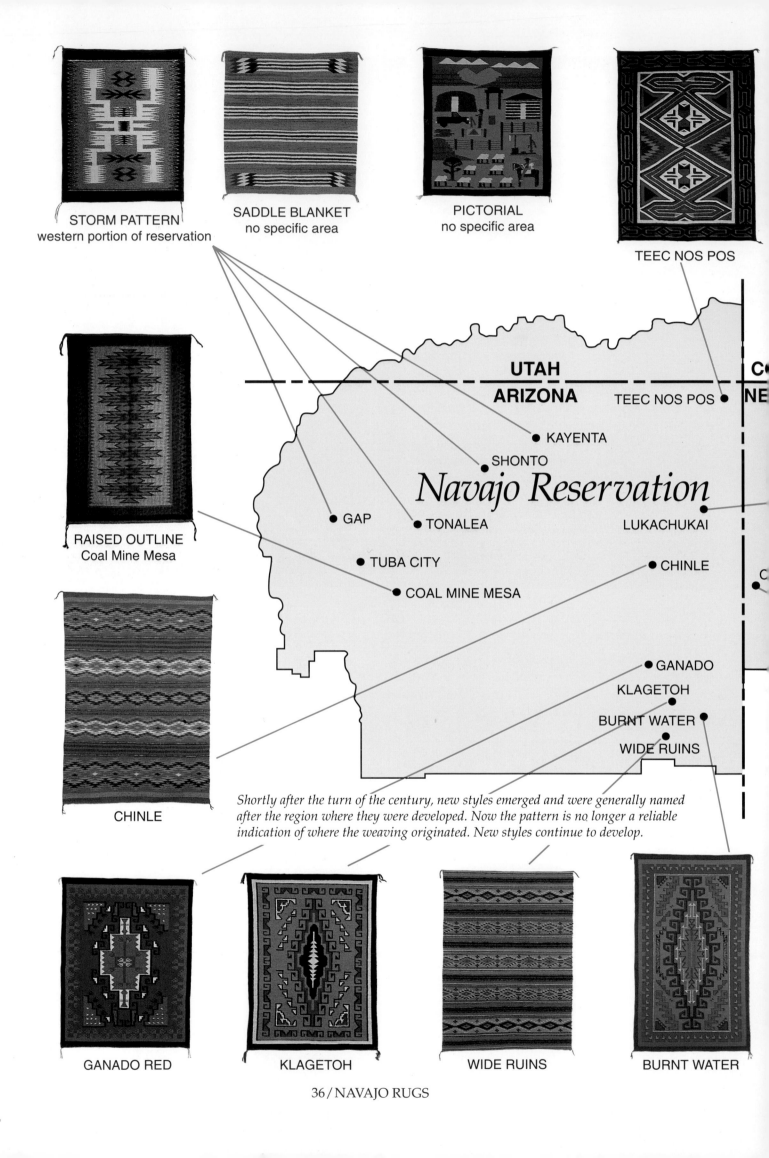

STORM PATTERN
western portion of reservation

SADDLE BLANKET
no specific area

PICTORIAL
no specific area

TEEC NOS POS

RAISED OUTLINE
Coal Mine Mesa

CHINLE

UTAH

ARIZONA

TEEC NOS POS

Navajo Reservation

KAYENTA

SHONTO

GAP   TONALEA

LUKACHUKAI

TUBA CITY

CHINLE

COAL MINE MESA

GANADO

KLAGETOH

BURNT WATER

WIDE RUINS

Shortly after the turn of the century, new styles emerged and were generally named after the region where they were developed. Now the pattern is no longer a reliable indication of where the weaving originated. New styles continue to develop.

GANADO RED

KLAGETOH

WIDE RUINS

BURNT WATER

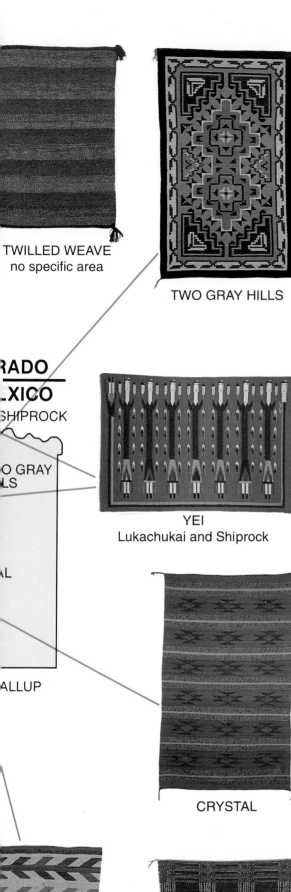

TWILLED WEAVE
no specific area

TWO GRAY HILLS

RADO
EXICO
SHIPROCK

O GRAY
LS

AL

ALLUP

YEI
Lukachukai and Shiprock

CRYSTAL

THROW
Gallup area

TWO-FACE
no specific area

Navajo textile artists have long used their weavings to reflect and comment about what goes on around them—and that has accelerated in this century as change has accelerated. Gwendolyn Nez chose to remember the Long Walk, when the U.S. Army force-marched the Navajo in 1864 to imprisonment far from their homeland. It was four years before they were allowed to return. Only a few Navajo managed to elude the army.

the Navajo were well-known for their weaving skills. Even the Spanish territorial government conceded that Navajo weaving surpassed that being produced by the best Spanish weavers.

From the 1700s through the late 1800s, Navajo women wove blankets that were highly prized and traded throughout the Southwest and beyond. The introduction of machine-woven blankets in the late 1800s began a decline in the quantity of Navajo weaving, with a consequent rise in the bags of wool from Navajo flocks exported to the East. That reversed when traders found a more profitable market in selling wool as rugs to the tourists who were then beginning to come out West on the Santa Fe Railroad. The new market was for floor rugs rather than wearing blankets, and weavers were paid by the pound, depending upon the grade, which was determined by the fineness of the weave.

There were changes as well in patterns, with large geometric designs with borders replacing the earlier banded styles. All of the regional styles we are familiar with today, such as Ganado and Two Gray Hills, began after the turn of the century. Traders began to encourage weavers to go back to finer weaves and experiment with more vegetal dyes, which have in turn been replaced by commercial dyes that match those colors.

A TIME-CONSUMING PROCESS

The casual visitor seldom realizes the hours of labor involved in making a rug. Traditionally it begins with the shearing of the wool, cleaning, carding, washing, dyeing, and more spinning. The amount of time spent in spinning determines the fineness of the weave. Yarn preparation easily exceeds the time spent in weaving for a tapestry-quality example. For this reason processed wool and commercially spun wool are becoming more prevalent.

When one includes the time spent setting up the loom, the entire procedure can result in a 3 x 5-foot rug of average quality (about 8 warp and 25 weft threads per inch) that required between 300 and 400 hours of work, depending upon the intricacy of the design. The same size textile, executed in a tapestry weave of about 25 warp and 80 weft threads per inch, would require in excess of 2,000 hours work by a master weaver.

The "spirit line" is used only by some weavers. Stories purporting to explain it vary wildly between weavers and traders. Basically, if the design is too symmetrical, the eye can be "trapped" looking for a variation. The spirit line "lets the eye out."

Once used for saddle blankets and personal wear, Navajo weaving was re-directed towards floor rugs and decorative wall hangings around the turn of the century. It has since been recognized as a textile art and used much as one would paintings.

Like those who weave baskets, no rug weaver can truly earn a living at her craft. The very best weavers generally command scarcely more than the equivalent of minimum wage for their work. Navajo weaving skills are still being passed down to the younger women (only a very few men weave), but the craft is surviving as an avocation rather than an occupation. It is the cultural importance more than the financial aspect that keeps the craft alive among the Navajo.

THE FUTURE OF NAVAJO RUGS

Navajo rugs are justly famous not only for their beauty, but also for their durability. It is the hand-spun yarn with its natural lanolin, which traditional processes leave in the yarn, that helps give these rugs their strength. It is not uncommon for a Navajo rug, given proper care, to last 30 to 40 years on the floor. However, today rugs are more commonly used as wall hangings than as floor coverings.

The demise of Navajo rugs has been predicted as imminent for over a century, and the end is not yet in sight—for either the weaving or the predictions. The craft is still being learned by young Navajo women, though many weave only a few rugs—often for their own use and enjoyment rather than for sale.

With each passing year the quantity of weavings declines somewhat, but the quality remains high. A few weavers produce rugs so fine that they far surpass the best of the pre-1900 textiles. Design innovations continue, but the regional styles have begun to blur: a Ganado rug may be woven not only at Ganado, but anywhere on (or off) the reservation. Navajo weavings also remain a popular trade item and prestige symbol among the tribes themselves.

Navajo Sandpainting Art

According to Navajo philosophy, the Universe is a very delicately balanced place full of enormously powerful forces. If the balance is upset it can cause illness or other disasters. It is believed that only humans can upset this balance. Should someone fall ill, a Navajo Chantway must be given to restore the patient to harmony. The particular chantway will depend upon the cause of the illness. For example, painful, swollen joints may be determined to have resulted from offending a bear, and the Mountainway will be prescribed.

These ceremonies, which may last from one to nine days, include prayers, medicinal herbs, songs, and sandpaintings under the guidance of a *hatathli,* or medicine man. The patient ceremonially identifies with the hero of the chantway to gain the hero's strength. Health returns as *hozho,* balance or harmony, is restored.

The sandpaintings, called *ikaah,* used in these ceremonies are created between sunrise and sunset of the same day. Until the mid-1950s only photographs or painted reproductions served as

a permanent record of these creations. It was then that the new craft began to evolve.

Sand is acquired by grinding up rock found at a number of locations within the traditional—as opposed to the modern legal—boundaries of Navajoland. After grinding, sifting, and grading the sand, the background sand is sprinkled across a sheet of particle board that has been prepared by the sandpainter with a specially mixed and thinned white glue.

The sandpainter uses the same glue and a fine paintbrush to begin the design. Working freehand, each color is applied separately, allowing plenty of time between colors for drying in order to avoid any blurring or mixing. The flow of sand is regulated by placing a pinch of sand in the palm of one hand and allowing it to trickle out between the index finger and the thumb. A soft, even flow over a glue line that is neither too thick nor too thin is necessary for an even line. After the sandpainting is completed and dry, the entire surface is usually sprayed with a very fine mist of shellac for additional protection.

Hatathlis warn that duplicating religious images can cause an illness to befall the maker. For this reason many who use a significant number of elements from religious sandpaintings will deliberately make certain changes, such as altering a color sequence or deleting a significant detail.

Since the mid-1970s Navajo sandpainting artists have been turning increasingly to non-religious subjects, including landscapes, portraits, still lifes, and abstracts. The artists are presently refining and expanding their techniques, taking on more elements of fine art.

Sometimes mistakenly referred to as Sun and Eagle, this sandpainting represents Pollen Boy on the Sun.

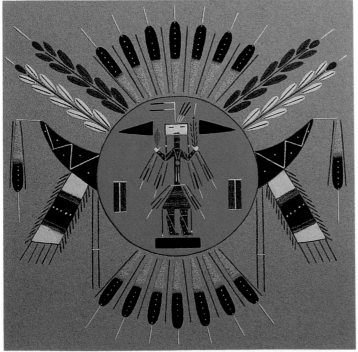

K. C. DEN DOOVEN

Many Navajo sandpainting artists use elements from the larger, more complex images that are a part of traditional Navajo healing ceremonies. Navajo hatathli or healers do not necessarily approve of this practice. For that reason, and to express personal creativity and vision, many younger artists are moving into other subject areas and developing and perfecting new techniques.
Eugene Baatsoslanii Joe

Baskets

Basketry is the oldest of all the present-day crafts. The importance of baskets in the religious activities of the many tribes is great, and exceeds any monetary consideration. From a purely economic standpoint, Indian basketry should have disappeared completely years ago. The hours involved in weaving a basket are considerable, yet a weaver can expect to earn little more than a dollar or two an hour for her labor. Even the finest baskets by the most skillful weavers sold directly to museums or collectors will net the weaver no more than the equivalent of minimum wage.

Even among tribes in which basket weaving has disappeared, baskets are in demand, creating a lively trade for weavers from tribes that still produce them. Most Navajo curing rites require the use of a basket in some portion of the ceremony. The Hopi present coiled basketry plaques to winners of footraces, and baskets of all sorts are used in the Basket Dance held in the fall. Sifter baskets are still in use in many Hopi households.

The Apache puberty rites, held for a young woman who has come of age, generally include one or more burden baskets. Baskets may be used in some pueblos as partial payment for ceremonial work performed. Among many tribes cornmeal is placed in the baskets for use as a prayer offering or blessing during religious ceremonies.

Few people appreciate baskets as do the Indians, who fully realize the time and skill that go into creating them. A basket weaver must know the seasons for gathering her materials (like rug weaving, it is primarily a woman's activity)

Basic coiled basketry involves a coil that is stitched together. This Tohono O'odham basket uses bear grass for the coil and bleached yucca for the stitching.

Much of the time in basket weaving is the gathering and preparation of materials. For Tohono O'odham baskets that means gathering bear grass from certain areas, yucca from other regions of their land, and devil's-claw seed pods, available only one time during the year. Preparation includes trimming, splitting, and soaking.

Hopi weavers use the greatest variety of basketry techniques, including coiling, plaiting, and twining. Villagers on Third Mesa weave willow wicker baskets, while those on Second Mesa make coiled baskets; all the villagers make yucca plaited baskets. Baskets are traded between villages, used in religious ceremonies and for special occasions, and sold or traded to non-Hopi.

and the places where they grow. It is not unusual for a Tohono O'odham weaver to travel 50 to 100 miles to gather a specific plant for her basketry. Additionally she must harvest, dry, preserve, and prepare the plants for use. Preparing the materials can include bleaching, dyeing, soaking, stripping, and trimming. Only then can the equally time-consuming task of actually weaving the basket begin.

STYLES OF BASKETS

The Rio Grande pueblos of New Mexico produce relatively few baskets, primarily plaited yucca baskets from Jemez and openwork willow baskets at a few other pueblos, notably Santo Domingo.

The Indians of Arizona produce a great quantity and diversity of basketry. The Hopi of Third Mesa make wicker trays, bowls, and plaques of rabbitbrush dyed with either vegetal or aniline

The number of O'odham basket weavers has been increasing over the last few decades, as has the number of baskets produced and the creativity in the designs used. Severely depressed economic conditions on their main reservation provide very limited job opportunities. As little as a basket weaver makes at this time-consuming craft (significantly less than minimum wage), it often represents the only alternative. Basketmaking is also part of efforts by the O'odham people to preserve their culture—material and spiritual—by passing down traditional skills and knowledge to each new generation.

dyes. Second Mesa villagers produce tightly woven coiled plaques of grass coils sewn with narrow strips of dyed yucca. The villagers of all three mesas make plaited yucca sifter baskets woven over a willow ring, a style that dates back over 1,500 years. Many weavers now use a metal ring for greater strength and durability. Occasionally the Hopi also weave plain plaited willow baskets for use as piki bread trays, peach baskets, and cradleboards. The Hopis themselves are the greatest consumers of their own basketry, but they do produce a surplus for sale or trade.

The Tohono O'odham of southern Arizona weave more baskets than all the other tribes in the United States combined. The craft was slowly declining in quantity in the 1950s when the American Friends Service Committee, involved in a struggle to help the O'odham acquire the mineral rights to their own land, helped stimulate basketmaking by encouraging weavers to

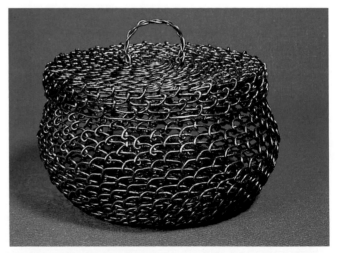

Traditionally made of baling wire, this type of basketry dates to the late 1800s. Handled baskets were often used to keep perishable food cool by lowering it into a well. Only a few weavers—mostly men—make them.

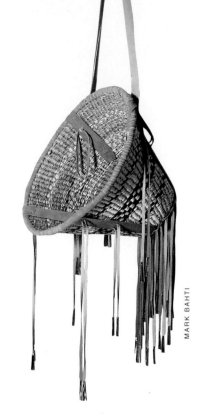

The tinklers on Apache burden baskets made noise to avoid startling bears while carrying heavy loads in their mountainous homelands.

pass on their skills, and by broadening the market for their craft. In 1963, an estimated 8,000 baskets were produced by weavers ranging in age from under 10 to over 80. In 1985, it was estimated that over 30,000 baskets had been woven. It is expected that a better economic situation will cause the number of baskets produced to eventually level off and ultimately decline.

Covered stitch baskets of yucca, or more rarely cattail, coils sewn with devil's claw, yucca, or even willow are occasionally seen, as are the more common baskets of bear grass coils sewn in an open stitch with yucca. Miniature baskets of horsehair, which have their origins around 1930, are also woven in considerable quantity.

The Tohono O'odham's neighbors to the north, the Pima, also produce baskets similar in both design and technique, though they use willow rather than yucca to stitch the coils, which are also made of willow. Very few weavers are still active among the Pima, and designs used by the Pima are now increasingly being woven by Tohono O'odham basket makers.

The Western Apache, famous for their tightly

Horsehair used to make ropes also became a source of material for miniature baskets beginning around the 1930s. Though good eyesight is required, little time is needed to prepare the material for weaving.

Beaded baskets date back to the late 1800s. The beading is done after the basket is complete rather than during weaving. Some Ute beading is done on baskets woven by artists of other tribes, notably the Tohono O'odham. Photographed at Notah–Dineh Trading Post

Years ago Jicarilla Apache willow baskets, with their bright aniline-dyed colors, were expected to eventually disappear. Instead, a modest revival has taken place. Photographed at Jicarilla Apache Tribal Co-op

Paiute willow baskets have also undergone a revival. In addition to traditional Paiute designs, weavers have created new ones and also responded to market demands by creating baskets using patterns from tribes whose baskets are disappearing or are no longer made. Photographed at Bill Beaver's Sacred Mountain Trading Post

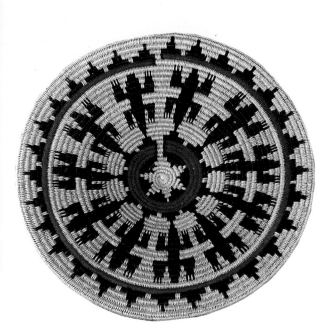

Navajo weavers, working in sturdy, durable willow,
are also experimenting with and creating new designs.
They sometimes incorporate elements of older motifs. The basket
to the right, commonly called a "wedding" basket, is a type used in many ceremonies.

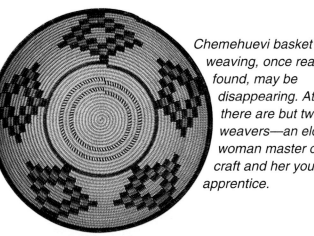

Chemehuevi basket
weaving, once readily
found, may be
disappearing. At present
there are but two
weavers—an elderly
woman master of the
craft and her young
apprentice.

woven, intricately designed willow coiled baskets, produce primarily twined willow burden baskets today. These are decorated with long buckskin fringe, usually with metal tinklers attached at the bottom. A few pitch-covered *tus,* or water baskets, are also made. The Jicarilla Apaches of northern New Mexico still make a few bright aniline-dyed coiled willow baskets.

The Havasupai, Hualapai, and Chemehuevi still produce baskets, but in very limited quantity. In northwest Mexico, along the desert coast of the Sea of Cortez, the Seri Indians weave coiled baskets of *torote* dyed with vegetal and aniline dyes. Metal pots and pans have replaced baskets in daily life since the 1960s. The Seri continue to weave baskets, however, because of the demand from American collectors for their beautiful, exceptionally sturdy baskets.

Basket prices are determined by the fineness of weave (number of stitches and coils per inch), symmetry, complexity of design, size, and shape, as well as materials, with willow being more durable but more difficult to work with than yucca. Understandably, the more time and skill that go into them, the more they will cost.

Willow wicker baskets are still woven in several
Rio Grande pueblos and by a few Mexican-American weavers.
Andrew Harvier

Hopi Katsina Carvings

The Hopi word *katsina* is used in three ways. It may refer to the actual spirit being, the impersonation by Hopi men in religious dances, or the painted, carved, wooden figurines.

The importance of the katsina in the religious life of the Pueblo people is indicated by the numerous depictions of their masks on pottery vessels and baskets, in kiva murals, and as petroglyphs on canyon walls throughout the Southwest. Today katsinas appear in ceremonies of most pueblos, but are more prevalent among the Hopi and Zuni villages. Among the Zuni, katsinas are known as *kokko*.

The katsina is a very old concept and though made far more frequently today, the *katsin tihu* or katsina doll probably extends back to the pre-Columbian era. Early Spanish missionaries believed them to be a form of idolatry, and reported confiscating and burning a large number in the Rio Grande pueblos. These dolls are not idols, nor are they worshipped or prayed to. Similarly they are not toys. They are used in the religious training of young Hopi children, and traditionally were given to women of childbearing years to help ensure fertility. The children and women receive the dolls as gifts or blessings from the masked katsina dancers who appear in the village during katsina ceremonies.

Non-Indians are often astonished to learn that the Hopi have well over 200 katsinas and cannot imagine why there is a need for so many. Similarly, some Hopi are astounded that there are over 1,000 saints in the Catholic faith. This comparison is somewhat appropriate in that some of the functions of the saint and the katsina are roughly parallel. Each serves to intercede on

In the past 20 years carvers have begun to work in more detail and with better tools. Unlike the earlier style, many pieces are now largely crafted from a single piece of wood. In this Pahi-Ala *katsina hand-carved of cottonwood root by Robert Sakhomenewa Albert, only the rattle and bow were carved separately and attached.*

K. C. DEN DOCVEN

Though there are fixed elements that must be included to correctly portray any given katsina, the work of carvers also reflects their individual artistic styles.

Some carvers utilize a sculptural style, meant more to represent the katsina spirit, while others prefer a more detailed approach that represents the katsina dancer.

To evoke the feeling of a particular katsina, great detail in carving and painting is not necessary as this old-style So-wing or Deer katsina by Philbert Honanie illustrates. Once disdained by collectors, their consequent disappearance from the market has fueled interest in a revival of the old style.

The Kwahu *or Eagle*
katsina is one of the
most popular katsina
dolls among collectors;
yet it is rarely seen in
ceremonies, and even
then usually appears in
a very different form.
It is a popular doll
among carvers wishing
to showcase their talent.
Henry Naha

This Palhik Mana *or Butterfly
Maiden is done in the style
that one would have
seen in the latter part of
the 1800s. The butterfly
was important not only
because it is so beautiful
but because it is one of
the few pollinators of
crops in Hopiland. Her
tablita incorporates cloud,
rain, rainbow, and corn motifs.*

Koshares *are one of several types of clowns that can appear during Hopi ceremonies to amuse and instruct by using their extreme behavior to reinforce Hopi values. This one by Lee Chapella is just plain lost.*

behalf of mortals with the more important deities. Persons unfamiliar with Pueblo Indian culture sometimes find the katsina dolls grotesque in appearance, but many tribes had a similar reaction to their first view of a crucifix.

Katsinas can be the spirits of birds, animals, places, objects, forces of nature, insects, plants, and even other tribes. Some are named for what they represent such as the *Nuvak* or Snow katsina, and the *Hon* or Bear katsina. Often the name cannot be translated, such as the *Qöqöle*. A katsina may also be named for its distinctive call, as is the case with the *Hololo* katsina.

Many of the katsinas have well-defined functions such as disciplining children, or opening the kivas at the Winter Solstice. A few, like the Bear, are credited with the power to cure specific ailments. One group, the *tsuku* or clowns, perform antics for the spectators. These

performances do more than simply relieve the solemnity of the occasion—they also reinforce certain rules of Hopi behavior through their humorously excessive acts.

The *Wawas Katsinam* or runner katsinas may challenge the men of the village to footraces and reward them with a basket if they win. If the katsina wins the loser may be switched, his hair cut, or his face rubbed with soot, depending upon which runner he lost to. These katsinas, along with some of the soyoko or "ogre" katsinas, also perform the task of keeping spectators at a proper distance and singling out those behaving inappropriately.

Katsinas are believed to live on the San Francisco Peaks north of Flagstaff, Arizona. At the time of the Winter Solstice, they leave their home to visit the Hopi villages where they dance for the residents. Their main objectives

There are several hundred katsinas, depending upon who is counting and how they are counting. The exact number seems to be more important to non-Hopi than Hopi. Their appearances can vary somewhat from mesa to mesa and a few appear only at certain villages. Their functions can also vary depending upon the religious ceremony in which they appear. From left to right these are: Hozro Wuuhti (Cold-Bringing Woman), Koyemsi (Mudhead), Qöqöle, Hilili, Pookonghoya, Kocha Hon (White Bear), Wakas (Cow), Tawa (Sun), Avats'hoya (Spotted Corn), and Anuthlona. Not all have names that can be translated, and some commonly accepted English names are not accurate.

are to ensure the continuation of the life cycle of all living things and to promote the general well-being of the people. Benefits are not limited to the Hopi, for they believe that a katsina dance, performed in the proper spirit, extends its blessings beyond the borders of their land. The katsina religious cycle ends in late July with the *Niman* or Home Dance, which marks the return of the katsinas to their mountain home until the next Winter Solstice.

Hopi men (a few women have begun to carve in the past 20 years) carve katsina figures from the root of the cottonwood tree. Using a variety of carving tools (including hand-held electric tools in some cases) and files they form the figure and then sand it smooth. Sandpaper and emery paper have replaced the traditional piece of sandstone for smoothing. The figure is then coated with either gesso or kaolin, a white clay, to seal the wood. Mineral and vegetal paints were traditionally used; however, much to the dismay of non-Hopi buyers, they rubbed off too easily when the figures were handled. The artists then began to use tempera and poster paints, which in turn were replaced by acrylic paints in the 1960s. Both the poster paints and the acrylics also offered a wider range of colors

than the traditional mineral and vegetal paints. Since 1990 several carvers have gone back to the more muted traditional pigments, with some using an acrylic base as a fixative.

THE SIGNIFICANCE OF COLORS

The colors with which a katsina is painted can be significant. The Hopi assign a different color for each of the six directions: yellow for the north, white for the east, red for the south, blue-green for the west, black for the zenith, and spotted or all colors for the nadir. Certain katsinas can appear with different directional-colored masks, or the color can simply be part of the name as with the *Sakwa Hu* or Blue Whipper.

Similarly, the feathers used are significant. Certain katsinas and their dolls are decorated with the feathers from specific birds. Feather use on katsinas that are sold is restricted by the Fish and Wildlife Service to most (but not all) species of domestic fowl, sparrow, quail, parrot, pigeon, and pheasant. Even feathers from most game birds cannot legally be used, causing most carvers to make feathers from wood instead.

Katsina figures range from the simple *putska tihu* or flat dolls, sometimes called cradle dolls, that are given to infants, to elaborately

Hopis receive their first doll or tihu *when in infancy. ("Doll" is a misleading word as they are not played with like toys.) The style of doll they are given is a* putska tihu *or flat doll. Traditionally this was also the type given to women of childbearing age during the katsina rites. Hopi boys traditionally no longer received dolls after they had been initiated into the Katsina Society. From left are:* Hahai Wuuhti, Susopa *(Cricket), and* Qöqöle. *Hahai Wuuhti is one of two regarded as being the grandmother of the katsinas. She is also usually the first putska tihu a Hopi infant is given.*

carved and painstakingly painted figures in action poses created basically from a single piece of wood—with virtually nothing added or glued on. Most katsina dolls have arms and accessories, such as bows or rattles, that are carved separately and then attached to the body with pegs and glue. Beginning in the 1980s a sculptural style has evolved, meant to evoke more the katsina spirit than the katsina dancer.

A particular katsina can differ in appearance from one village or mesa to the next. In fact, some known at one may not appear at all in another. This variance has led to the mistaken belief that Hopi carvers deliberately leave out certain details on katsinas that are carved "for sale." This is generally untrue. Detail and proportions of a katsina will vary depending upon the carver's skill and style of work, and be reflected in the price, but in Hopi eyes skill does not make for a "better" doll—only accuracy in its depiction is important.

Pottery

A new pottery tradition—the making of storyteller figurines—has arisen to commemorate an old tradition—that of the storyteller who passed on the traditions and beliefs of the tribe to succeeding generations. Chris and Vera Fragua

The art of pottery making in the Southwest is nearly 2,000 years old. Early pieces were used as cooking pots, water jars, storage jars, and ceremonial vessels. Both form and design varied from one tribe to the next, just as they do today. Change was the rule rather than the exception. Archaeologists employ a chronology based upon progressive changes in Pueblo pottery types as a method of dating prehistoric sites.

Introduction of metal containers had a profound effect on the ceramic arts. By the early 1900s large storage jars were infrequently produced, and the use of cooking vessels had sharply declined. At the same time, demand by non-Indians for smaller, more decorative pieces increased and pottery production was tailored to fit the new market.

Most modern Southwest Indian pottery is made in the same manner as prehistoric ware. Clay is dug from local deposits and ground, soaked, refined, and mixed with a grit or temper.

Most pottery construction is by the coil and scrape method—building the vessel by coiling long ropes of clay into the desired shape and then pinching them together. Next the vessel is scraped smooth with a piece of gourd or metal to obliterate any sign of the coils. A few tribes, such as the Tohono O'odham, use a paddle and anvil technique, by which the pieces of clay are flattened and molded piece by piece to build the vessel. The potter's wheel was never used by traditional Indian potters.

Often a coat of clay, called a clay slip, is applied. The slip is a mixture of water and very fine clay which is painted or wiped over the surface of the pot. Then, depending upon the pueblo, the surface may be polished with a small, smooth stone. If there are to be painted designs they are

Since its beginning at Cochiti in 1964, the making of storyteller figurines has spread to other pueblos in the Rio Grande Valley and west to Acoma, where this one was made by Corinne Garcia. Each pueblo has a unique general style range within which artists express their individuality.

The Tewa potters have long made a carved ware but only since the 1960s have they employed a technique called sgraffito. This technique differs from earlier methods in two distinct ways: it is shallower and it is done after the piece has been polished and fired. Tse-Pe

applied at this point. Specific designs and colors used depend largely on the potter's tribal affiliation, though stylistic boundaries are beginning to break down. Experimentation and innovation continue, with the creation of new designs and the borrowing or resurrection of older, often prehistoric designs, as well as the reinterpretation of those early designs. The painting, in either mineral or vegetal paints, is usually applied with a brush made of yucca, though a few potters now use conventional paintbrushes.

FIRING OF THE POTTERY

After it dries, the pottery is fired by placing it on a grate or bed of potsherds around which a wood fire is lit. In some cases the pottery is covered with sheet metal (usually tin) and large shards, and a fire is built under and around the pottery. Dried dung, usually sheep manure, is often used for firing, although coal or wood are also used by some Pueblo potters. The firing itself generally lasts no more than a few hours from start to finish, with temperatures ranging from 850 to 1,300 degrees Fahrenheit—higher for coal-fired kilns.

Pottery fired in this manner is fairly porous. Glazes were known in prehistoric times but were used exclusively for decoration, not

(continued on page 60)

TAOS-PICURIS—The micaceous clay used by potters from these villages gives their pottery a golden glitter. This ware is well-fired, and their wide-mouthed bean pots are much sought after for use as cooking vessels.

SAN JUAN—The most common types are a plain polished redware, a light brown incised ware made of a clay that contains mica, and a polychrome. Some pieces are carved in low-relief.

SANTA CLARA—Styles include polished red and blackware, carved, sgraffito, or with matte paint designs, and a polychrome redware with blue-gray and white designs, as well as some white-slipped polychrome ware. Animal, bird, and human figurines are also made.

SAN ILDEFONSO—Highly polished red and blackware with matte paint designs were revived by the renowned potter Maria Martinez beginning in the 1920s. Carved ware was begun in the early 1930s and sgraffito work in the 1960s. A little polychrome redware is occasionally produced. Pottery from Santa Clara and San Ildefonso are identical in appearance.

POJOAQUE—Pottery here has been revived in recent years much as the pueblo itself was resettled and revived over 60 years ago. Micaceous ware, blackware, polychrome redware, and some carved ware and sgraffito are now produced here.

NAMBE—Micaceous clay pottery from this pueblo's pottery revival includes sculptural pieces as well as carved ware, polychrome ware, polished redware, and sgraffito work—similar to types produced at Santa Clara.

TESUQUE—The poster-painted, sun-dried pottery once associated with this pueblo has nearly disappeared. In its place is a rebirth of traditional pottery— some of it black on gray-white, a little polychrome, and some micaceous ware.

COCHITI—Storyteller figurines are the primary pottery form at this pueblo. Though they once produced bowls and jars, those have now nearly disappeared.

SANTO DOMINGO—Though best known for black on white with a red bottom, a little polychrome work is done, along with a matte on polished black and some black or polychrome on redware.

SAN FELIPE—The older style polychrome work has disappeared, but there are a few remaining potters who produce a black on red and a polished ware made from mica-flecked clay.

JEMEZ—Known for years for its poster-paint and later its acrylic-paint pottery, this pueblo has undergone a major revival with sgraffito work, polished redware that includes black on red, cream on red and polychrome, a polychrome on cream, and figurative work including storytellers.

ZIA—Classic pottery from this pueblo is a black and red on a cream- or sand-colored slip with a red base, but a few potters use acrylic paints in executing intricate designs after firing.

ISLETA—Most of the pottery here is produced by two families and is primarily polychrome though a few potters have experimented with polished redware and sgraffito. Storytellers are also made.

LAGUNA—A Keresan-speaking Pueblo people like Acoma, their pottery, while limited in quantity, is very similar in appearance to classic Acoma pottery.

ACOMA—This pueblo produces very fine black on white, polychrome, and plain white—sometimes corrugated—ware. A few potters also make storytellers and figurines.

ZUNI—In the last two decades Zuni pottery has undergone a revival of its polychrome wares and figurative work. A few potters use a sand-colored slip rather than white and a number model small lizards and frogs atop their bowls.

NAVAJO—For more than 30 years Navajo pottery has edged away from near-disappearance of utility ware to a thriving craft, with several potters creating new styles— including a subtle polychrome, a "folk-art" style, and an exceptional polished ware—all coated with a pinyon pitch that is sometimes mistaken for a glaze.

HOPI—A range of types can be found here beginning with a redware, a whiteware, and a yellowware with either black or polychrome designs. Some plainware, corrugated pottery, painted tiles, and carved or sgraffito work are also made.

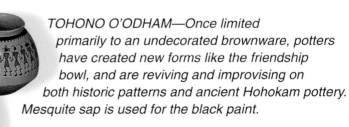

TOHONO O'ODHAM—Once limited primarily to an undecorated brownware, potters have created new forms like the friendship bowl, and are reviving and improvising on both historic patterns and ancient Hohokam pottery. Mesquite sap is used for the black paint.

European missionaries affected the religious life of the Pueblo Indians, as exemplified by this nativity scene by Andrew Harvier. However, despite their best efforts, much of traditional Pueblo beliefs and practices continues, with selected Christian practices and beliefs being incorporated into their older lifeway.

waterproofing. A porous pot used for water storage allows for the evaporation of moisture seeping through the sides, which cools the water inside the jar. In southern Arizona, water jars made by the Tohono O'odham were popular for this reason and used by residents of towns in southern Arizona until after the turn of the century.

Black and red polished ware from the Tewa pueblos of Santa Clara and San Ildefonso owe their colors primarily to two different methods of firing. To achieve a polished red finish the smoothed pot is coated with a red clay slip, polished, and then fired in an oxidizing atmosphere where the air is allowed to freely circulate and the fire burns cleanly. For the black finish, the same slip is applied and polished, but the pot is then fired in a reducing atmosphere in which the fire is smothered and a dense smoke created. The carbon in this smoke is absorbed by the iron oxide in the clay and "locked in." It will not rub off.

The traditional method of firing is filled with potential pitfalls. If the ground is too damp, or the wind comes up, or the pottery is exposed too soon to a cold atmosphere, or if there is a sudden change in the weather while firing, or there is an air pocket in the clay wall of a pot, the entire kiln-load of pottery, representing weeks or even months of work, can be ruined.

Some pottery produced for the non-Indian tourist trade is sun-dried or simply oven-baked rather than fired, and then painted with poster paint or acrylic paint, but it is less often seen these days. Its more modern counterpart is greenware— a commercially produced, mold-made pot—paint-

Whether creating bowls for serving stew or one-of-a-kind masterpieces bound for private art collections, the basic techniques remain the same. Lonnie Vigil

ed with commercial paints, which may be applied either before or after firing.

Other recent changes in pottery making include *sgraffito* (a carving technique employed after firing), secondary firings to create two-toned pots, new mineral paints and glazes, gas or electric kilns and, occasionally, the potter's wheel. A few potters even add turquoise, coral, or shell beads to highlight their design work, or draw upon old design traditions to create highly individualistic work that exhibits great skill and artistry.

Buying Indian Crafts

With few exceptions, the first Indian-owned and operated Indian arts businesses were primarily tribal guilds and coops opened shortly after World War II. A growing number of Indian entrepreneurs—some of them artists—are now opening their own shops. Adelphia Martinez, Elvis Torres

Every art has its imitators, and Indian art is no exception. Its broad appeal makes Indian jewelry the craft most often imitated. Misleading advertising is responsible for much of the fraud perpetrated on the public. The words "Indian design" or "Indian style" are no guarantee that the items are Indian handmade. In fact, they usually indicate the opposite. Similarly, "silver metal" and "turquoise-blue stones" are simply descriptive terms that a careless buyer may misinterpret. "Reservation-made" is another meaningless phrase, for an Indian handmade item is no more or less authentic for having been created on or off a reservation.

Beware of major "discounts" as they are usually meaningless. The Indian artisans normally have a set price—the only variable is the store's markup. A store that quadruples its jewelry prices can offer a 50 percent discount that winds up being the same as the regular price of a store that doubles but does not "discount."

A purchase made directly from an Indian is not always a guarantee of authenticity either. Many an imitation has been bought from a genuine Indian by unwary buyers. A person who would never consider buying a diamond from a street-corner vendor will not hesitate to buy an imported Indian-style rug or a pair of earrings if the seller is picturesque enough.

As with any craft there are shortcuts that artisans can take that influence the value. There is also an extensive range of imitations and imitation materials. Obviously no one can become an expert on Indian crafts in a short period of time. Therefore it is necessary to rely upon dealers who have a reputation for handling authentic crafts. The Indian Arts and Crafts Association in Albuquerque, New Mexico, museums, and even the craftspeople themselves can be good sources to inquire about the names of reputable shops. A few Indian tribes operate guilds or cooperatives that are also good places to buy the crafts of that tribe.

Another way to become a careful, informed shopper, is to familiarize oneself with Indian crafts by attending some of the many exhibitions of Indian art held in the Southwest, and asking questions of the traders and craftspeople. State offices of tourism can be contacted for specific places and dates.

Even the most knowledgeable buyer is well-advised to obtain all claims in writing on the receipt. Certificates of authenticity are no guarantee but, like a well-written receipt, they can provide the basis for a refund if the item turns out not to be as claimed.

In recent years many Indian artists have become the focus of brochures, articles, and other promotional material. Many will list awards, ribbons, and recognition they have received for their work. While this can be an indication that you are looking at the work of a talented artist, some exceptionally fine artists choose not to enter competitions and shun the limelight or have been ignored by it. Additionally, a famous artist can have a bad day and an unknown artist can have a moment of glorious inspiration. Buy a piece because *you* like it, not because the salesperson, a crafts judge, or a magazine writer likes it.

The suggested reading list at the end of this book can provide additional information to assist the reader in becoming a more knowledgeable, discriminating buyer, and to develop an appreciation and understanding of not only Southwestern Indian arts and crafts, but Southwestern Indian culture as well.

Care of Indian Crafts

Silver jewelry usually has areas that have been deliberately oxidized, or darkened, to heighten the contrast that creates the design. If this patina is accidentally removed, it can be restored by using a little "liver of sulfur" mixed in a bit of water and applied with a toothpick or small paintbrush. Craft shops sell this and other solutions for oxidizing jewelry. Allow it to dry before polishing the raised areas.

Some people like a high polish on their jewelry while others like the softer patina that comes with age and use. To restore the polish, use a jeweler's rough cloth. Paste can get caught in the recessed areas, and dips can harm the stones and remove all the oxidation. Household ammonia, applied carefully with a Q-tip, can remove heavy tarnish.

To avoid continually bending a bracelet, which will cause it to eventually crack and break, put it on just above the wrist bone from the inside of the arm. Then rotate it over the wrist. To take it off, reverse the procedure. The bracelet should fit loosely enough to be comfortable without falling off.

When putting on a bracelet, especially one set with stones, one must exercise care to avoid bending the bracelet. It should be put on from the inside of the arm, just above the wrist bone, with a rolling motion. To take it off, simply reverse the action. If a bracelet is bent, even slightly, each time it is taken on and off, it will crack and eventually break. Bending will also crack or loosen the stones in their settings.

Stones set in bezels usually have a cushion of either sawdust or a bit of cardboard to help absorb minor impacts without cracking. If it is immersed in water the backing can swell, causing the stone to loosen and fall out. Inlaid stones can be susceptible to soaps and oils loosening their bond with the epoxy that holds them in place. Coral, as well as medium to soft grades of turquoise, can also be harmed by repeated exposure to soaps and oils.

Silver bead necklaces, including squash blossom necklaces, are best strung on foxtail—a braided steel wire.

Heishe should be strung on braided nylon. Monofilaments (single strands of nylon or wire) and fine silver chains do not wear well·or last long. Very fine necklaces may be strung on silk thread. Care should be taken to avoid contact with water and oils, which might shrink or weaken the stringing material.

Navajo rugs should never be shaken clean as the snapping motion tends to fray the ends and break the warp threads. Vacuuming is preferable. Floor rugs should be turned end for end and reversed from time to time to ensure even wear and mellowing of the colors. They should also have a rubber pad—preferably a waffle pad—to prevent slipping and reduce wear and tear.

Navajo rugs that are hung should also be turned end for end and reversed periodically as this not only ensures that any mellowing of the color over the years occurs uniformly, but also provides an opportunity to check for the presence of bugs that might harm the weaving. Hangings should be mothproofed annually and vacuumed regularly.

The best way to hang a Navajo rug is with Velcro™. A strip of the wide, self-adhesive hook side of Velcro™ can be applied either directly to the wall or to a strip of wood, which is then hung from the wall. When the rug is pressed against it, the thousands of tiny nylon hooks catch and hold the rug. If the rug is older there may not be enough nap left for the Velcro™ to hold. Specially designed, often decorative, wooden clamps are made that permit hanging the rug without sewing or otherwise piercing it.

If a rug is to be stored for any length of time it should be mothproofed and then rolled to avoid creases from folding. Also, it is best wrapped in a clean white sheet rather than plastic. If the rug needs a spot removed, take it to a cleaner who handles fine oriental textiles, as Navajo rugs require the same type of care and attention in the cleaning process. Navajo rugs can be dry-cleaned, but the harsh chemicals can leave the wool fibers brittle over time, which can shorten the life of a rug intended for floor use.

Indian baskets can be hung by using thread or a bit of fine wire. Hold the basket up to the light and with an awl or needle enlarge two holes to run the wire or thread through. If the basket is so tightly woven that no light shines through, then carefully select two points in between the coils and in between the stitches. This is advisable only for new baskets, not older baskets that have become somewhat brittle. To use a basket for serving bread or fruit, line it with a napkin. Avoid hanging the basket where it might receive direct sunlight that can fade or discolor it, or near

The best way to hang a Navajo rug is using the hook side of Velcro™. This will allow you to easily attach and remove the rug. If it has been used on a floor, however, there may not be enough nap to hold it.

a kitchen where it can absorb cooking oils from the air and discolor.

Traditional *Indian pottery* should not be used as a planter unless a glass jar is used as a liner; otherwise the moisture will seep through the pot and begin to blister and disintegrate the design and the surface itself. In order to prevent the bottom of the pot from marring a table, or erasing the potter's signature through wear, place it on a felt or buckskin pad. Dust with a very light touch and only with a clean, dry cloth.

Though some Indian pottery was meant to hold water, it isn't fired at a high enough temperature to hold it without eventually sustaining damage. Those collecting it as art should keep it away from any moisture. Frequent or rough, careless handling can rub away the painted surface. Similarly, repeated handling of a fine pot can deposit oils from the skin on the surface, causing discoloration. Some damage can be restored by professionals, but the finish of polished Santa Clara pottery, for example, cannot be fully restored.

SUGGESTED READING

ADAIR, JOHN. *The Navajo and Pueblo Silversmiths*. Norman: University of Oklahoma Press, 1944.

BABCOCK, BARBARA and GUY and DORIS MONTHAN. *The Pueblo Storyteller*. Tucson: University of Arizona Press, 1986.

BAHTI, MARK and EUGENE BAATSOSLANII JOE. *Navajo Sandpainting Art*. Tucson, Arizona: Treasure Chest Publications, 1978.

BRANSON, OSCAR T. *Turquoise: Gem of the Centuries*. Tucson, Arizona: Treasure Chest Publications, 1975.

CUSHING, FRANK H. *Zuni Fetishes*. Expanded version by Mark Bahti. Las Vegas, Nevada: KC Publications, 1999.

DUNN, DOROTHY. *American Indian Painting of the Southwest and Plains Areas*. Albuquerque: University of New Mexico Press, 1968.

HEDLUND, ANN LANE. *Contemporary Navajo Weaving— Thoughts That Count*. Flagstaff: Museum of Northern Arizona, 1994.

HUCKO, BRUCE. *Southwestern Indian Pottery*. Las Vegas, Nevada: KC Publications, 1999.

JERNIGAN, WESLEY. *Jewelry of the Prehistoric Southwest*. Albuquerque: University of New Mexico Press, 1976.

MAXWELL, GILBERT. *Navajo Rugs: Past, Present and Future*. Santa Fe, New Mexico: Southwest Images [Revised Edition], 1984.

RODEE, MARIAN and JAMES OSTLER. *The Fetish Carvers of Zuni*. Albuquerque and Zuni, New Mexico: Maxwell Museum of Anthropology and the Pueblo of Zuni Arts and Crafts, 1995.

TANNER, CLARA LEE. *Southwest Indian Painting*. Tucson: University of Arizona Press, 1957.

TRIMBLE, STEVEN. *Talking with the Clay*. Santa Fe, New Mexico: School of American Research Press, 1987.

WHITEFORD, ANDREW HUNTER. *Southwestern Indian Baskets: Their History and Their Makers*. Santa Fe, New Mexico: School of American Research Press, 1988.

WRIGHT, BARTON. *Hopi Kachinas: The Complete Guide to Collecting Kachina Dolls*. Flagstaff, Arizona: Northland Press, 1977.

A Jemez figurine by Maxine Toya of a woman in traditional garb and the hairstyle of a Pueblo maiden.

The Publisher gratefully acknowledges the use of original paintings from the following galleries and museums: Amerind Foundation, Inc.; James T. Bialac Collection; Elvis Torres Gallery; Simons Collection; and Oliver Enjady's private collection. Items photographed in this Southwestern Indian Trilogy came from numerous shops, museums, private collections, and individual Indian artisans. The work represents the broad range of items available for sale at reputable Indian arts and crafts shops nationwide.

Books on Indian Culture and the Southwest: Southwestern Indian Arts and Crafts, Southwestern Indian Tribes, Southwestern Indian Ceremonials, Southwestern Indian Pottery, Canyon de Chelly, Monument Valley, Mesa Verde, Grand Circle Adventure, The Rocks Begin to Speak, The Southern Paiutes, The Navajo Treaty, Zuni Fetishes. A hardbound edition combining the first 3 Southwestern Indian books is also available.

Other Series by KC Publications:
The Story Behind the Scenery - on America's national parks.
in pictures - companion series on America's national parks.
 • **Translation Packages available.**
Voyage of Discovery - on the expansion of the western United States.

NEW! WildLife @ Yellowstone.

To receive our catalog with over 115 titles:

Call **(800-626-9673)**, fax **(702-433-3420)**, write to the address below, Or visit our web site at **www.kcpublications.com**

Published by KC Publications, 3245 E. Patrick Ln., Suite A, Las Vegas, NV 89120.

Inside back cover: The Mongwa *or Owl katsina of the Hopis by Robert Sakhomenewa Albert Photo by Bruce Hucko*

Back cover: Navajo sandcast buckle on Navajo rug Photo by K. C. DenDoover

Created, Designed, and Published in the U.S.A
Ink formulated by Daihan Ink Co., Ltd
Printed by Doosan Corporation, Seoul, Korea
Color Separations by Kedia/Kwang Yang Sa Co., Ltd
Paper produced exclusively by Hankuk Paper Mfg. Co., Ltd